the guide to owning a
Staffordshire L

Marion Lane

T.F.H. Publications, Inc.
One TFH Plaza
Third and Union Avenues
Neptune City, NJ 07753

Copyright © 2003 by T.F.H. Publications, Inc.

All rights reserved. No part of this publication may be reproduced, stored, or transmitted in any form, or by any means electronic, mechanical or otherwise, without written permission from T.F.H. Publications, except where permitted by law. Requests for permission or further information should be directed to the above address.

Printed and Bound in China
07 08 09 10 11   3 5 7 9 8 6 4 2

ISBN13 978-0-7938-1880-8

This book has been published with the intent to provide accurate and authoritative information in regard to the subject matter within. While every precaution has been taken in preparation of this book, the author and publisher expressly disclaim responsibility for any errors, omissions, or adverse effects arising from the use or application of the information contained herein. The techniques and suggestions are used at the reader's discretion and are not to be considered a substitute for veterinary care. If you suspect a medical problem, consult your veterinarian.

The Leader In Responsible Animal Care For Over 50 Years!™
www.tfh.com

Contents

A Staffordshire pup can grow into your best friend if given the proper care.

The History of the Staffordshire Bull Terrier

Walk a Staffordshire Bull Terrier down the street and you are bound to be asked this question: "Is that a Pit Bull?"

Most Stafford owners are quick to answer no, and then take the time to say the name of the breed over and over, slowly and carefully, to make sure there is no misunderstanding. They may go on to try to explain what a Pit Bull actually is: "bigger," "longer legs," "cropped ears," "vicious," "trained to fight."

The Staffordshire Bull Terrier is often mistaken for a Pit Bull, since it was once bred as a fighting dog.

However, the complete and correct answer to the question would be not "no," but "not anymore." At one time the Staffordshire Bull Terrier was a so-called Pit Bull—a dog bred and conditioned to fight other dogs in an enclosure called a pit. In fact, the Staffordshire Bull Terrier was the original pit fighting dog, from which others have descended. But that was over a hundred years ago. Today the Staffordshire Bull Terrier, both here and in England, is a family pet.

ORIGIN OF THE BREED

In England in the early 1800s an unspeakably inhumane spectator sport called bullbaiting was in vogue. This bloody spectacle called for a tethered bull to be first roused to a fury by tormenting humans and then to be attacked by a succession of large, aggressive dogs. In combating the bull, the dog would attempt to attach itself to the bull's nose and then hold on despite the bull's violent efforts to shake and toss it off. The type of Bulldog (not to be confused with our modern "sourmug" Bulldog) most successful in fighting bulls weighed between 80 and 100 pounds, had a powerful neck and shoulders, and tremendous courage and tenacity. Its lower jaw tended to protrude somewhat to allow the Bulldog to continue breathing without loosening its grip until the bull was pinned to the ground. Large purses were offered to encourage the best Bulldogs from surrounding areas to compete.

Then, in 1835, bullbaiting became illegal. This left promoters and partisans of the "blood sports" to come up with something to take its place. The new spectacle was dog fighting.

At first the Bulldogs were pitted against one another, but it soon became obvious to dog fighters that a smaller, more agile dog would be better suited for dog-to-dog combat. They crossed the Bulldog with one or more of the native English terriers in an attempt to create a type of dog that would combine the courage, strength and tenacity of the Bulldog with the agility and fire of the terrier. The plan worked, and a consummate fighting dog was the result. The new breed went by many names: Bull and Terrier, Half and Half, Pit Dog, Pit Bullterrier and—for the region where it originated—Staffordshire Bull Terrier.

OVERCOMING THE PAST

Dog fighting in turn was declared illegal in England, but the difficulty of enforcement only served to drive it underground at first. In the meantime, a huge surge of interest in legitimate dog shows and exhibitions, on both sides of the Atlantic, was taking place. At least some owners of Staffordshire Bull Terriers were interested in this new venue for showing off their dogs, but because of its unsavory past, the breed was not accepted for registration in the

THE GUIDE TO OWNING A STAFFORDSHIRE BULL TERRIER

The American Kennel Club officially recognized the Staffordshire Bull Terrier as a breed in 1975.

Kennel Club of England until 1935. It was approved for registration in the American Kennel Club in 1975.

Over 20 years later, the Stafford remains a relatively rare breed in the US. For the year 1995, only 372 were registered. By and large the breeders and fanciers of the Stafford are very happy with this state of affairs. Considering what the breed has had to endure in its first 160 years, it certainly doesn't need to fall into the hands of people who may not understand and appreciate it.

During the many long years that Staffordshire Bull Terriers were active fighting dogs, breeders had little interest in any qualities other than their fighting abilities. But meanwhile, almost coincidentally, the dogs had been developing many fine characteristics that contributed to their success in the pit but also made them excellent all-

around family dogs. Possibly the most important of these is the dog's unusual affection for the human race in general. This quality seems surprising until you learn that the rules of pit fighting eliminated from competition any dog that attacked a person in the pit—all the more astonishing when you consider that almost any dog, in the heat of a squabble with another dog, may very well bite his owner if he tries to intervene.

A second quality that ironically was enhanced by pit fighting was the Stafford's overwhelming desire to please its owner. It has been reported that during an actual fight, the owners of the combatants would continually move around the enclosure to make sure they were always in their dog's line of sight. Sadly, it seemed to be the encouragement of its owner that gave an exhausted dog the heart to continue.

Characteristics of the Staffordshire Bull Terrier

One of the best ways to find out what a Stafford is like is to ask people who have never owned one themselves but have spent time with others who have. Why should this be so? Because try as they might, owners can't be objective. And when it comes down to it, they make all breeds sound alike: "intelligent," "loyal," affectionate," "great with the kids," "hates the mailman." Doesn't that just about describe every dog that's ever lived?

The Staffordshire Bull Terrier is still an uncommon breed in the US.

With the Staffordshire Bull Terrier such an uncommon breed in this country, most people who see one for the first time do not know what it is. Nevertheless, they think they do: they think it's one of those vicious Pit Bulls. It may take more than the owner's assurance to convince them that it isn't, but once they've let go of the idea, they can begin to discover with delight what the Stafford really is:

"My, he's so strong!" This comment usually follows the first tentative pat on the dog's shoulder. It should be obvious to the most casual observer that the Stafford is packed with muscles, but most people are not prepared for just how strong the dog really is. If they volunteer to walk him on lead, their amazement will be even more profound.

"This is a first!" There's genuine surprise in the veterinarian's voice. Apparently the Stafford is the only dog who actually struggles and strains to get inside the clinic door.

"Kelly, don't hurt the doggie." The three-year-old's mother is duly embarrassed. Her daughter Kelly has just hit the Stafford in the head with a tinker toy. Meanwhile, the Stafford is patiently squinting her eyes against the next assault.

"Whoa!" This is the surprised shout of the person who chose to ignore the owner's warning that his male Stafford didn't like other males. It occurred as he was hastily hauling his

Your Staffordshire Bull Terrier loves to be cuddled by his family. Take time to show your pup that he's loved.

barking dog out of the face of the snarling one. Staffords should not be expected to like strange dogs, especially ones that are insolent enough to run right up to them.

"Excellent!" The teenage boy whistles in admiration as the Stafford leaps straight up in the air from a sitting position.

"What a friendly dog!" This is the comment that most warms the heart because it so clearly reveals surprise. People really walk around believing these dogs are vicious.

"And be sure to bring the dog!" The ultimate compliment. Friends and relatives include the Stafford in all invitations. "Never even know he's around," they say.

The Standard for the Staffordshire Bull Terrier

General Appearance—The Staffordshire Bull Terrier is a smooth-coated dog. It should be of great strength for its size and, although muscular, should be active and agile.

Size, Proportion, Substance—Height at shoulder: 14 to 16 inches. Weight: Dogs, 28 to 38 pounds; bitches, 24 to 34 pounds, these heights being related to weights.

Height for a Staffordshire Bull Terrier should be 14 to 16 inches at the shoulder. Dogs should weigh from 28 to 38 pounds and with bitches being between 24 and 34 pounds.

The Staffordshire Bull Terrier comes in many different colors and combinations of colors.

Non-conformity with these limits is a fault. In proportion, the length of back, from withers to tail set, is equal to the distance from withers to ground.

Head—Short, deep through, broad skull, very pronounced cheek muscles, distinct stop, short foreface, black nose. Pink (Dudley) nose to be considered a serious fault. *Eyes*—Dark preferable, but may bear some relation to coat color. Round, of medium size, and set to look straight ahead. Light eyes or pink eye rims to be considered a fault, except that where the coat surrounding the eye is white the eye rim may be pink. *Ears*—Rose or half-pricked and not large. Full drop or full prick to be considered a serious fault. *Mouth*—A bite in which the outer side of the lower incisors touches the inner side of the upper incisors. The lips should be tight and clean. The badly undershot or overshot bite is a serious fault.

Neck, Topline, Body—The neck is muscular, rather short, clean in outline and gradually widening toward the shoulders. The body is close coupled, with a level topline, wide front, deep brisket and well sprung ribs being rather light in the loins. The tail is undocked, of medium length, low set, tapering to a point and carried rather low. It should not curl much and may be likened to an old-fashioned pump handle. A tail that is too long or badly curled is a fault.

The Staffordshire's legs should be straight and well boned. They should also be set rather far apart.

THE GUIDE TO OWNING A STAFFORDSHIRE BULL TERRIER

The Staffordshire is an active and agile dog with free and powerful movements.

Forequarters—Legs straight and well boned, set rather far apart, without looseness at the shoulders and showing no weakness at the pasterns, from which point the feet turn out a little. Dewclaws on the forelegs may be removed. The feet should be well padded, strong and of medium size.

Hindquarters—The hindquarters should be well muscled, hocks let down with stifles well bent. Legs should be parallel when viewed from behind. Dewclaws, if any, on the hind legs are generally removed. Feet as in front.

Coat—Smooth, short and close to the skin, not to be trimmed or de-whiskered.

Color—Red, fawn, white, black or blue, or any of these colors with white. Any shade of brindle or any shade of brindle with white. Black-and-tan or liver color to be disqualified.

Gait—Free, powerful and agile with economy of effort. Legs moving parallel when viewed from front or rear. Discernible drive from hind legs.

Temperament—From the past history of the Staffordshire Bull Terrier, the modern dog draws its character of indomitable courage, high intelligence, and tenacity. This, coupled with its affection for its friends, and children in particular, its off-duty quietness and trustworthy stability, makes it a foremost all-purpose dog.

Disqualification
Black-and-tan or liver color.
Approval November 14, 1989
Effective January 1, 1990

Your New Staffordshire Bull Terrier Puppy

SELECTION

When you pick out a Staffordshire Bull Terrier puppy as a pet, don't be hasty; the longer you study puppies, the better you will understand them. Make it your transcendent concern to select a puppy that radiates good health and spirit and is lively on his

Selecting the right puppy should not be a five-minute decision. Take your time and examine a number of pups before selecting the one for your family.

When transporting your Staffordshire by car, place him in a crate. The Nylabone® Fold-Away Pet Carrier is perfect for transporting your dog.

feet. He should have bright eyes and a shiny coat, and he should come forward eagerly to make and to cultivate your acquaintance. Don't fall for any shy little darling that wants to retreat to his bed or his box, or plays coyly behind other puppies or people, or hides his head under your arm or jacket appealing to your protective instinct. Pick the Staffordshire Bull Terrier puppy that forthrightly picks you. The feeling of attraction should be mutual!

DOCUMENTS

Now, a little paperwork is in order. When you purchase a purebred Staffordshire Bull Terrier puppy, you should receive a transfer of ownership, registration material, and other "papers" (a list of the immunization shots, if any, the puppy may have been given; a note on whether or not the puppy has been wormed; a diet and feeding schedule to which the puppy is accustomed; etc.). Along with these documents, you are welcomed as a fellow owner to a long, pleasant association with a most lovable pet.

GENERAL PREPARATION

You have chosen to own a particular Staffordshire Bull Terrier puppy. You have chosen him very carefully over all other breeds and all other puppies. So, before you have even gotten that adorable puppy home, you will have prepared for his arrival by reading everything you can get your hands on having to do with the management of the breed and the proper care of puppies. True, you will run into many conflicting opinions, but at least you will not be starting "blind." Read, study, and digest. Talk over your plans with your veterinarian, other "Staffordshire Bull Terrier people," and the breeder of your puppy.

When you get your Staffordshire Bull Terrier puppy, you will find that your reading and study are far from finished. You've just scratched the surface in your plan to provide the greatest possible comfort and health for him; and, by the same token, you do want to assure yourself of the greatest possible enjoyment of this wonderful creature. You must be ready for this puppy mentally, as well as in the physical requirements.

TRANSPORTATION

If you take the puppy home by car, protect him from drafts, particularly in cold weather. Wrapped in a towel and carried in the arms or lap of a passenger, the Staffordshire Bull Terrier puppy will usually make the trip without mishap. If the pup starts to drool and to squirm, stop the car for a few minutes. Have newspapers handy in case of carsickness. A covered carton lined with newspapers provides protection for puppy and car, if you are driving alone. Avoid excitement and unnecessary handling of the pup on arrival. A Staffordshire Bull Terrier puppy is a very small "package" that will be making a complete change of surroundings and company, and he needs frequent rest and refreshment to renew his vitality.

THE FIRST DAY AND NIGHT

When your puppy arrives in your home, put him down on the floor and don't pick him up again, except when it is absolutely necessary. He is a dog, a real dog, and must not be lugged around like a rag doll. Handle him as little as possible, and permit no one to pick him up and baby him. To repeat, put your puppy on the floor or the ground and let him stay there except when it may be necessary to do otherwise.

Quite possibly, your Staffordshire Bull Terrier puppy will be afraid in his new surroundings for a while, especially without his mother and littermates. Comfort him and reassure him, but don't console him. Don't give him the "oh-you-poor-itsy-bitsy-puppy" treatment. Be clam, friendly, and reassuring. Encourage him to walk around and sniff over his new home. If it's dark, put on the lights. Let him roam for a few minutes while you and everyone else concerned sit quietly or go about your routine business. Let the puppy come back to you.

Give your new puppy plenty of time to become adjusted to his new home. He'll adapt fast and become the perfect pup.

Playmates may cause an immediate problem if the new Staffordshire Bull Terrier puppy is to be greeted by children or other pets. If not, you can skip this subject. The natural affinity between puppies and children calls for some supervision until a responsible relationship is established. This applies particularly to a "Christmas puppy," because this is a time when there is more excitement than usual and more chance for a puppy to experience something upsetting. It is a better plan to welcome the puppy several days before or after the holiday week. Like a baby, your Staffordshire Bull Terrier puppy needs much rest and should not be overhandled. Once a child realizes that a puppy has "feelings" similar to his own and can readily be hurt or injured, the opportunities for play and responsibilities provide exercise and training for both child and pet.

For his first night with you, your pup should be placed where he is to sleep every night—say, in the kitchen, because the floor can usually be easily cleaned. Let him explore the area to his heart's content; close doors to confine him there. Prepare his food, and feed him lightly the first night. Give him a bowl with some water in it—not a lot, since most puppies will try to drink the whole bowl dry. Give him an old coat or shirt to lie on. Because a coat or shirt will be strong in human scent, the pup will pick it out to lie on, thus furthering his feeling of security in the room where he has just been fed.

HOUSETRAINING HELPS

Sooner or later—mostly sooner—your new Staffordshire Bull Terrier puppy is going to "puddle" on the floor. First, take a newspaper and lay it on the puddle until the urine is soaked up onto the paper. Save this paper. Next, take a cloth with soap and water, wipe up the floor and dry it well. Then, take the wet paper and place it on a fairly large square of fresh newspapers in a convenient corner. When cleaning up, always keep a piece of wet paper on top of the others. Every time he wants to "squat," he will seek out this spot and use the papers. (This routine is rarely necessary for more than three days.) When you have done this, leave your Staffordshire Bull Terrier puppy in his space for the night. Quite probably, he will cry and howl a bit; some are more stubborn than others on this matter. However, let him stay alone for the night. This may seem harsh treatment, but it is the best procedure in the long run. Just let him cry; he will soon weary of it.

Feeding Your Staffordshire Bull Terrier

Let's talk about feeding your dog, a subject so simple that it's amazing there is so much nonsense and misunderstanding about it. Is it expensive to feed a Staffordshire Bull Terrier? No, it is not! You can feed him economically and keep him in perfect shape the year round, or you

Your dog does not need variety when being fed. Constantly changing your dog's diet will lead to digestion problems.

can feed him expensively. He'll thrive either way, so let's see why this is true.

First, remember that a Staffordshire Bull Terrier is a dog. Dogs do not have a high degree of selectivity in their food, and unless you spoil them with great variety (and possibly turn them into poor, "picky" eaters), they will eat almost anything to which they become accustomed. Many dogs flatly refuse to eat nice, fresh beef. They pick around it and eat everything else. But meat—bah! Why? They aren't accustomed to it!

VARIETY IS NOT NECESSARY

A good general rule of thumb is: Forget about all human preferences and don't give a thought to variety. Choose the right diet for your Staffordshire Bull Terrier and feed it to him day after day, year after year, winter and summer. But what is the right diet?

Hundreds of thousands of dollars have been spent in canine nutrition research. The results are pretty conclusive, so you needn't go into a lot of experimenting with trials of this and that every other week. Research has proven just what your dog needs to eat to stay healthy.

DOG FOOD

There are almost as many right diets as there are dog experts, but the basic diet most often recommended is one that consists of a dry food, either meal or kibble form. There are several of excellent quality, manufactured by reliable companies, research tested, and nationally advertised. They are inexpensive, highly satisfactory, and easily available in stores everywhere in containers of 5 to 50 pounds. Larger amounts cost less per pound, usually.

If you have a choice of brands, it is usually safer to choose the better known one; but even so, carefully read the analysis on the package. Do not choose any food in which the protein level is less than 25 percent, and be sure that this protein comes from both animal and vegetable sources. The good dog foods have meat meal, fish meal, liver, and such, plus protein from alfalfa and soybeans, as well as some dried-milk product. Note the vitamin content carefully. See that they are all there in good proportions; and be especially certain that the food contains properly high levels of vitamins A and D, two of the most perishable and important ones. Note the B-complex level, but don't worry about carbohydrate and mineral levels. These substances are plentiful and cheap and not likely to be lacking in a good brand.

The advice given for how to choose a dry food also applies to moist or canned types of dog foods, if you decide to feed one of these.

Having chosen a really good food, feed it to your Staffordshire Bull

Make sure your Staffordshire Bull Terrier has plenty of fresh, clean water, especially when he plays outside on warm days.

FEEDING YOUR STAFFORDSHIRE BULL TERRIER

Terrier as the manufacturer directs. Once you've started, stick to it. Never change the diet if you can possibly help it. A switch from one meal or kibble-type food can usually be made without too much upset; however, a change will almost invariably give you (and your Staffordshire Bull Terrier) some trouble.

WHEN SUPPLEMENTS ARE NEEDED

Now, what about supplements of various kinds, mineral and vitamin, or the various oils? They are all okay to add to your Staffordshire Bull Terrier's

If your dog requires supplements you can add them to his food.

food. However, if you are feeding your dog a correct diet, and this is easy to do, no supplements are necessary unless your dog has been improperly fed, has been sick, or is having puppies. Vitamins and minerals are naturally present in all the foods; and to ensure against any loss through processing, they are added in concentrated form to the dog food you use. Except on the advice of your veterinarian, added amounts of vitamins can prove harmful to your Staffordshire Bull Terrier! The same risk applies to minerals.

FEEDING SCHEDULE

When and how much food do you give your Staffordshire Bull Terrier? As to when (except in the instance of puppies), suit yourself. You may feed two meals per day or the same amount in one single feeding, either morning or night. As to how to prepare the food and how much to give, it is generally best to follow the directions on the food package. Your own Staffordshire Bull Terrier may want a little more or a little less.

Fresh, cool water should always be available to your dog. This is important to good health throughout his lifetime.

ALL DOGS NEED TO CHEW

Puppies need something with resistance to chew on while their teeth and jaws are developing—for cutting the

THE GUIDE TO OWNING A STAFFORDSHIRE BULL TERRIER

All dogs need to chew. Provide your dog with safe chew toys, such as those made by Nylabone®.

puppy teeth, to induce growth of the permanent teeth under the puppy teeth, to assist in getting rid of the puppy teeth at the proper time, to help the permanent teeth through the gums, to ensure normal jaw development, and to settle the permanent teeth solidly in the jaws.

The adult Staffordshire Bull Terrier's desire to chew stems from the instinct for tooth cleaning, gum massage, and jaw exercise—plus the need for an outlet for periodic doggie tensions.

This instinct is why dogs, especially puppies and young dogs, will often destroy property worth hundreds of dollars when their chewing instinct is not diverted from their owner's possessions. This is also why you should provide your Staffordshire Bull Terrier with something to chew—something that has the necessary functional qualities, is desirable from the dog's viewpoint, and is safe for him.

It is very important that your Staffordshire Bull Terrier not be permitted to chew on anything he can break or on any indigestible thing from which he can bite sizable chunks. Sharp pieces, such as from a bone that can be broken by a dog, may pierce the intestinal wall and kill. Indigestible things that can be bitten off in chunks, such as from shoes or rubber or plastic toys, may cause an intestinal stoppage (if not regurgitated) and bring painful death, unless surgery is promptly performed.

Strong natural bones, such as 4- to 8-inch lengths of round shin bone from mature beef—either the kind you can get from a butcher or one of the variety available commercially in pet stores—may serve your dog's teething needs if his mouth is large enough to handle them effectively. You may be tempted to give your puppy a smaller bone and he may not be able to break it when you do, but puppies grow rapidly and the power of their jaws constantly increases until maturity. This means that a growing dog may break one of the smaller bones at any time, swallow the pieces, and die painfully before you realize what is wrong.

All hard natural bones are very abrasive. If your dog is an avid chewer, natural bones may wear away his teeth prematurely; hence, they then should be taken away from your dog when the teething purposes have been served. The badly worn, and usually painful, teeth of many mature dogs can be traced to excessive chewing on natural bones.

Contrary to popular belief, knuckle bones that can be chewed up and swallowed by your dog provide little, if any, usable calcium or other nutriment. They do, however, disturb the digestion of most dogs and cause them to vomit the nourishing food they need.

The nylon bones, especially those with natural meat and bone fractions added, are probably the most complete, safe, and economical answer to the chewing need. Dogs cannot break them or bite off sizable chunks; hence, they are completely safe, and being longer lasting than other things offered for the purpose, they are economical. Nylabone® is highly recommended by veterinarians as a safe, healthy nylon bone.

Nothing, however, substitutes for periodic professional attention for your Staffordshire Bull Terrier's teeth and gums, not any more than your toothbrush can do that for you. Have your dog's teeth cleaned at least once a year by your veterinarian (twice a year is better), and he will be happier, healthier, and a far more pleasant companion.

Grooming Your Staffordshire Bull Terrier

The Staffordshire Bull Terrier is a dream to groom. Fifteen minutes a week should do it. Here are the essentials:

BRUSHING

Brush your Stafford with a rubber curry brush or natural bristle brush. Use pressure to stimulate the skin,

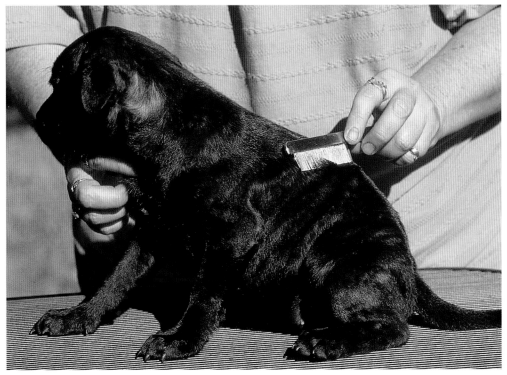

Although he doesn't require hours of grooming, your Staffordshire should be brushed a few times a week. Regular brushing will keep your dog's coat looking its best.

remove dead hair and bring a luster to the coat. During the shedding seasons, usually in the spring and fall, you may need to brush every second or third day to keep the hair in your house to a minimum. If you notice any dry skin or dandruff, your dog probably needs a bit more fat in his diet. A bath is not the answer. Speak to your veterinarian about a suitable supplement. Patches of hair loss, with or without scratching, should not be ignored. Some Staffords seem to be prone to localized mange as small puppies. The good news is that they usually outgrow it, even without any treatment.

BATHING

If your dog falls into a muddy hole, give him a bath. Use warm water and a baby shampoo or a shampoo made for dogs. Rinse well to get all the soap out of the coat. Towel off and allow to air dry, away from drafts. Unless the dog is truly dirty, he doesn't need a bath. On the other hand, a bath once or twice a year, whether he needs it or not, is probably a good idea just to keep the Stafford comfortable with the idea.

EAR CARE

Check your Stafford's ears weekly for dirt or wax. Wipe clean with cotton moistened with a little baby oil. You may use a cotton-tipped swab to clean the canal but be certain to insert the swab no further than you can see. Note the odor of the ear. A strong odor or discharge indicates an infection and should not be ignored.

EYE CARE

Keep an eye on your Stafford's eyes. Anything more than a very slight discharge that forms small crusts in the corner of the eye is abnormal. Redness in the whites of the eyes can mean allergies; discuss this with your veterinarian. Take note if your dog does any prolonged rubbing or pawing at his eyes. Staffords don't approach anything gingerly and an overzealous session of scratching or pawing can actually damage the cornea. If in doubt, have your dog examined by your veterinarian.

DENTAL CARE

Get in the habit of cleaning your Stafford's teeth once a day using a toothbrush and toothpaste made for dogs. Many dogs like the taste of the toothpaste and this process is not at all the ordeal it may sound. Another way to keep your dog's teeth healthy and clean is to provide a supply of safe, durable chew devices like Nylabones®. These strong bones are designed to give dogs an outlet for their chewing instinct and, at the same time, to strengthen and stimulate the jaws and gums, keeping the mouth healthy and plaque buildup to a minimum. Despite

Brush your dog's teeth regularly. If you notice excessive plaque or tartar buildup, contact your vet to have your dog's teeth cleaned.

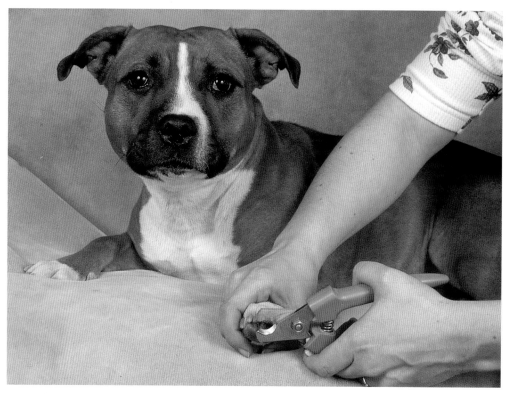

Dogs that regularly exercise outside may never need to have their nails trimmed. If you keep your dog indoors, clip his nails on a weekly basis.

regular cleaning, your dog may still need periodic cleaning by your veterinarian. The telltale signs of brown stains on the teeth and offensive breath odor mean it's time for a professional cleaning.

NAIL TRIMMING

If you exercise your Stafford regularly you may never need to trim his nails. However, it's a good idea to do so on a regular basis, even if you only remove a tiny shaving. Dogs in general do not like having their feet handled or their nails clipped, and it's important to keep them accustomed to the procedure. To clip your Stafford's nails, use a nail clipper made for dogs and remove only the very tip where the nail curves down. Inside each nail there is a blood vessel, called the "quick," which extends almost to the end of the nail. If you cut into this vessel by accident, it will both bleed and hurt, and cutting the dog's nails in the future will be much more difficult. To be on the safe side, ask your veterinarian or a professional groomer to show you how to cut the nails before you try it on your own.

Training Your Staffordshire Bull Terrier

When you added a Staffordshire Bull Terrier to your family, you probably wanted a companion and a friend. You may have wanted a dog to go for walks, take jogs, or play with your children. To do any of these things, your puppy will need training.

Good basic training will transform your jumpy, squirmy, wiggly little puppy into a well-mannered Staffordshire Bull Terrier that is a joy to be around. A trained puppy won't jump up on people, dash out the open door, or raid the trashcan. He will be able to be all you want him to be. Your puppy needs to have someone tell him what to do. Your Staffordshire Bull Terrier has the right to be trained—it is unfair to leave him to figure out the human world on his own, and he won't be able to do it.

You, too, will benefit from training, because you will learn how to moti-vate your dog, how to prevent problem behavior, and how to correct mistakes that do happen. Puppy training entails much more than learning the traditional sit, down, stay, and come commands—it means that you will be teaching your puppy to live in your house. You can set some rules and expect him to follow them.

HOUSEHOLD RULES

Start teaching your puppy the household rules as soon as possible—preferably as soon as you get him home. Your eight- to ten-week-old puppy is not too young to learn what you expect of him. When you teach him these rules from the start, you can prevent bad habits from forming.

When deciding what rules you want him to follow, picture your puppy as the adult dog you want him to be. Take a practical look at your puppy and your environment and decide what behavior you can or cannot live with. It is important to make these decisions early in your dog's life, because what he learns as a puppy will remain with the adult dog.

HOUSETRAINING

One of the first things that you will undertake will be housetraining your Staffordshire Bull Terrier. You are teaching your dog that he has a specific place that he should eliminate, preferably outside. Your best bet is to start housetraining him as soon as possible. However, you need to remember that puppies between the ages of 8 to 16 weeks do not have control of their bladders or bowels. They are not able to "hold it" until they get a little older, which means that in the beginning, housetraining will take vigilance on your part. You will have to watch very carefully for signs that your puppy needs to eliminate. He will usually have to go to the bathroom after eating, drinking, sleeping, and playing. Most puppies will also give off signals, like circling or sniffing the floor. These behaviors are a sure sign that your puppy needs to go outside. When you see him display this behavior, don't hesitate. Carry your pup outside to the spot where you want him to eliminate. Praise your dog for eliminating in the proper spot.

CRATE TRAINING

With the help of a regular schedule, you will be able to predict the times that your puppy will need to potty. The most useful thing that you can buy for your puppy to help facilitate this process is a crate. Training your puppy to use a crate is the quickest and easiest way to housetrain him. Remember that your Staffordshire Bull Terrier will be developing habits throughout his training that will last him his lifetime—make sure you teach the right ones.

By about five weeks of age, most puppies are starting to move away from their mom and littermates to relieve themselves. This instinct to keep the bed clean is the basis of crate training. Crates work well because puppies do not want to soil where they eat and sleep. They also like to curl up in small dark places that offer them protection on three sides, because it makes them feel more secure. When you provide your puppy with a crate, you are giving him his very own "den"—to your puppy's inner wolf, it is home sweet home. Pups will do their best to eliminate away from their den, and later, away from your house.

Being confined in the crate will help a puppy develop better bowel and bladder control. When confined for gradually extended periods of time, the dog will learn to avoid soiling his bed. It is your responsibility to give

Housetraining is easier for your puppy if you always bring him back to the same spot. He will learn that this is his potty area and seek it out when he needs to go.

The Nylabone® Fold-Away Pet Carrier makes the ideal crate for your dog. Make sure that there is a comfy blanket and some chew toys in it to keep your dog busy.

your dog plenty of time outside the crate and the house, or the training process will not be successful.

Sometimes puppies really just need to get away from it all. The hustle and bustle of a busy household can be overwhelming at times. There are times when your puppy will get overstimulated and need to take a "time out" to calm down (especially if you have rambunctious kids around). A crate is great for all of these times. The crate can be used as your puppy's place of refuge. If he's tired, hurt, or sick, he can go back to his crate to sleep or hide. If he's overstimulated or excited, he can be put in his crate to calm down. If you are doing work around the house that doesn't allow you to watch over him, you can put him into his crate until you are done painting the bathroom or the workmen have left. In short, crates are lifesavers for puppy owners. Eventually, the puppy will think that it is pretty cool, too.

CHOOSING A CRATE

There are many different types of crates to choose from. Consider what you will be using the crate for and pick the best one. The Nylabone® Fold-Away Pet Carrier is ideal because it folds away for easy storage when your dog is not using it. It is also good to use for traveling, especially by air, and some dogs feel more secure in an enclosed space.

The wire crates provide more ventilation in hotter weather and more room to move around.

A crate is an expensive item, and you will want it to last, so buy a crate that will fit your dog's adult size. An adult dog should be able to stand up, turn around, and stretch out in the crate comfortably. However, you don't want your little puppy to have too much room to roam around in, either. This might become a problem, because he may decide to eliminate in one corner of his big, roomy crate and sleep in the other. The best thing to do is to block off a portion of the crate and make it progressively larger as your dog matures and grows.

INTRODUCING THE CRATE

Introduce your puppy to the crate very gradually. You want the puppy to feel like this is a pleasant place to be. Begin by opening the door and throwing one of your puppy's favorite treats inside. You may want to teach him a command, like "bedtime" or "crate" when the pup goes into the crate. Let your dog investigate the crate and come and go freely. Don't forget lots of praise. Next, offer a meal in the crate. Put the food dish inside and after awhile, close the door behind him. Open the door when he's done eating. Keep this up until your puppy eats all his meals in the crate.

Soon your puppy will become accustomed to going in and out of the crate for treats and meals. If you do not wish to continue feeding him in his crate, you can start feeding elsewhere, but continue offering a treat for going into the crate. Start closing the door and leaving your puppy inside for a few minutes at a time. Gradually increase the amount of time your puppy spends in the crate. Always make sure that you offer him a treat and praise for going in. It is also a good idea to keep a few favorite toys inside the crate as well.

CRATE DON'TS

Don't let your puppy out of the crate when he cries or scratches at the door. If you do, your dog will think that complaining will bring release every time. The best thing to do for a temper tantrum is to ignore the pup. Only open the door when the dog is quiet and has calmed down.

Don't use the crate as punishment. If you use the crate when he does something bad, your dog will think of the crate as a bad place. Even if you want to get the pup out of the way, make sure that you offer him lots of praise for going into the crate and give a treat or toy too.

CRATE LOCATION

During the day, keep your puppy's crate in a location that allows him easy access and permits him to be

This Staffordshire pup is right at home sleeping under his master's chair.

THE GUIDE TO OWNING A STAFFORDSHIRE BULL TERRIER

part of the family. The laundry room or backyard will make a dog feel isolated and unhappy, especially if he can hear people walking around. Place it anywhere the family usually congregates—the kitchen or family room is often the best place.

At night, especially when your puppy is still getting used to the crate, the ideal place for it is in your bedroom, near your bed. Having you nearby will create a feeling of security and be easier for you as well. If the pup needs to go outside during the night, you can let him out before he has an accident. Your dog will also be comforted by the smell, sight, and sound of you, and will be less likely to feel frightened.

OUTSIDE SCHEDULE

As was mentioned before, puppies need time to develop bowel and bladder control. The best way to most accurately predict when your Staffordshire Bull Terrier needs to eliminate is to establish a routine that works well for both of you. If you make a daily schedule of eating, drinking, and outside time, you will notice your puppy's progress.

Every person and family will have a different routine—there is no one right schedule for everyone. Just make sure that you arrange times and duties that everyone can stick with. The schedule you set will have to work with your normal routine and

lifestyle. Your first priority in the morning will be to get the puppy outdoors. Just how early this will take place will depend much more on your puppy than on you. Once your puppy comes to expect a morning walk, there will be no doubt in your mind when he needs to go out. You will also learn very quickly how to tell a puppy's "emergency" signals. Do not test the young puppy's ability for self-control. A vocal demand to be let out is confirmation that the house-breaking lesson is learned.

It is also important to limit your puppy's freedom inside the house and keep a careful eye on him at all times. Many puppies won't take the time to go outside to relieve themselves because they are afraid that they will miss something; after all, everything exciting happens in the house. That's where all the family members usually are. Unfortunately, you may find your puppy sneaking off somewhere—behind the sofa or to another room—to relieve himself. By limiting the puppy's freedom, you can prevent some of these mistakes. Close bedroom doors and put baby gates across hallways. If you can't supervise him, put the dog in the crate or outside in a secure area.

ACCIDENTS WILL HAPPEN

When housetraining your dog, remember that if the puppy has an accident in the house, it is not his fault, it's yours. It means that the puppy was not supervised well enough or wasn't taken outside in time.

If you catch your dog in the act, don't yell or scold him. Simply say "No!" loudly, which should startle and stop him. Pick your pup up and go outside to continue in the regular relief area. Praise your puppy for finishing outside. If you scold or punish him, you are teaching him that you think going potty is wrong. Your dog will become sneaky about it, and you will find puddles and piles in strange places. Don't concentrate on correction; emphasize the praise for going potty in the right place.

If you find a little surprise left for you, do not yell at your puppy for it and never rub his nose in it. Your puppy will have no idea what you are talking about, and you'll only make him scared of you. Simply clean it up and be sure to keep a closer eye on him next time.

Housetraining is one of the most important gifts that you can give your dog. It allows him to live as one of the family. Every puppy will make mistakes, especially in the beginning. Do not worry—with the proper training and lots of patience, every dog can be housetrained.

BASIC TRAINING
Collar and Leash Training
Training a puppy to a collar and leash is very easy and something you can start doing at home without assistance. Place a soft nylon collar on the puppy. The pup will initially try to bite at it, but will soon forget it's there, more so if you play with him. Some people leave their dog's collar on all of the time; others put it on only when they are taking the dog out. If it is to be left on, purchase a narrow or round one so it does not mark the fur or become snagged on furniture.

Once the puppy ignores his collar, you can attach the leash to it and let him pull it behind him for a few minutes every day. However, if the pup starts to chew at the leash, simply keep it slack and let the pup choose where to go. The idea is to let your dog get the feel of the leash, but not get in the habit of chewing it. Repeat this a couple of times a day for two days, and the pup will get used to the leash without feeling restrained.

Next, you can let the pup understand that the leash will restrict his movements. The first time this happens, your dog will either pull, buck, or just sit down. Immediately call the pup to you and give him lots of praise. Never tug on the leash or drag the puppy along the floor. This might cause the puppy to associate his leash with negative consequences. After a few lessons, the puppy will be familiar with the restrictive feeling, and you can start going in a direction

Make sure that your dog is wearing his leash and collar whenever you take him outside.

The sit command should be an easy one for your dog to learn. If he is having difficulty learning the sit, place him in the correct position as you say, "Sit."

THE GUIDE TO OWNING A STAFFORDSHIRE BULL TERRIER

opposite from the pup. Give the leash a short tug so that the pup is brought to a halt, call the pup to you enthusiastically, and continue walking. When the puppy is walking happily on the leash, end the lesson with lots of praise. There is no rush for your puppy to learn leash training, so take as long as you need to make the dog feel comfortable.

Basic Commands

Although your puppy should attend puppy kindergarten, begin training as soon as your puppy is comfortable in your home and knows his name. It is also very helpful to take the lessons that you learn together in kindergarten and practice them at home. Doing your homework together will not only reinforce what you learn in class, it will allow you to spend some quality one-on-one time with your pup.

There are two very important things to remember when training your puppy. First, train the puppy without any potential distractions. Second, keep all lessons very short. Eliminating any distraction is import-ant because it is essential that you have your puppy's full attention. This is not possible if there are other people, other dogs, butterflies, or birds to play with. Also, always remember that puppies have very short attention spans. Even when the pup has become a young adult, the maximum time you should train him would be about 20 minutes. However, you can give the puppy more than one lesson a day, three being as many as are recommended, each well apart. If you train any longer, the puppy will most likely become bored, and you will have to end the session on a down note, which you should never do.

Before beginning a lesson, always play a little game so that the puppy is in an active state of mind and more receptive to training. Likewise, always end lessons with play time for the pup, and always end training on a high note, praising the puppy. This will really build his confidence.

The Come Command

The come command is possibly the most important command you can teach your puppy—it may even save your dog's life someday. Knowing that your dog will come to you immediately when you call him will ensure that you can trust him to return to you if there is any kind of danger nearby. Teaching your puppy to come when called should always be a pleasant experience. You should never call your puppy in order to scold or yell at him or else he will soon learn not to respond. When the pup comes to you, make sure to give him a lot of praise, petting, and, in the beginning, a treat. If he expects happy things when he reaches your side, you'll never have trouble getting your dog to come to you.

Start with your puppy on a long lead about 20 feet in length. Have plenty of treats that your puppy likes. Walk the distance of the lead, and then crouch down and say, "Come." Make sure that you use a happy, excited tone of voice when you call the pup's name. Your puppy should come to you enthusiastically. If not, use the long lead to pull him toward you, continuing to use the happy tone of voice. Give him lots of praise and a treat when you puppy gets there. Continue to use the long lead until your puppy is consistently obeying your command.

The Sit Command

As with most basic commands, your puppy will learn the sit command in just a few lessons. One 15-minute lesson each day should do the trick in no time. Some trainers will advise you that you should not proceed to other commands until the previous one has been learned really well. However, a bright young pup is quite capable of handling more than one command per lesson and certainly per day. As time progresses, you will be going through each command as a matter of routine before a new one is attempted. This is so the puppy always starts, as well as ends, a lesson on a high note, having successfully completed something.

There are two ways to teach the sit command. First, get a treat that your dog really likes and hold it right by his nose, so that all his attention is focused on it. Raise the treat above his head and say, "Sit." Usually, the puppy will follow the treat and automatically sit. Give him the treat for being such a good dog and don't forget to praise him. After a while, the pup will begin to associate the word "Sit" with the action. Most puppies will catch on very quickly. Once your dog is sitting reliably with the treat, take it away and just use praise as a reward.

However, there are some puppies that are more stubborn than others. They may need a little more encouragement to get the picture. If your puppy doesn't sit automatically when the treat is over his head, place one hand on the pup's hindquarters and the other under his upper chest. Say, "Sit" in a pleasant (never harsh) voice, and at the same time, lightly push down on his rear end and push up under the chest until your dog is sitting. Give lots of praise and give the pup the treat. Repeat this a few times, and your pet will get the idea. Most puppies will also tend to stand up at first, so immediately repeat the exercise. When the puppy understands the command and does it right away, you can slowly move backward so that you are a few feet away. If he attempts to come to you, simply place the dog back in the original position and start again. Do not attempt to keep the pup in the sit

Training commands can begin almost as soon as you bring your new Staffordshire puppy home. Train him right from the beginning to make sure he follows your rules.

position for too long. Even a few seconds is a long time for a impatient, energetic puppy, and you do not want him to get bored with lessons before he has even begun them.

The Stay Command

The stay command should follow your sit lesson, but it can be very hard for puppies to understand. Remember that your puppy wants nothing more than to be at your side, so it will be hard for him to stay in one place while you walk away. You should only expect your dog to perform this command for a few seconds at first, and then gradually work up to longer periods of time.

Face the puppy and say, "Sit." Now step backward, saying, "Stay." It is also very helpful to use the hand signal for stay—place your hand straight out, palm toward the dog's nose. Let the pup remain in the position for only a few seconds before saying, "Come" and giving lots of praise and a treat. Once your dog gets the hang of it, repeat the command again, but step farther back. If the pup gets up and comes to you, simply go back to the original position and start again. As the pup starts to understand the command, you can move farther and farther back.

Once your puppy is staying reliably from a short distance, the next test is to walk away after placing the pup. This will mean your back is to the dog, which will tempt him to follow you. Keep an eye over your shoulder, and the minute the pup starts to move, spin around, say, "Stay," and start over from the original position.

As the weeks go by, you can increase the length of time the pup is left in the stay position—but two to three minutes is quite long enough for a puppy. If your puppy drops into a down position and is clearly more comfortable, there is nothing wrong with it. In the beginning, staying put is good enough!

The Down Command

From the puppy's viewpoint, the down command is one of the more difficult ones to accept. This position is submissive in a wild pack situation. A timid dog will roll over, which is a natural gesture of submission. A bolder pup will want to get up and might back off, not wanting to submit to this command. The dog will feel that he about to be punished, which would be the position in a natural environment. Once he comes to understand this is not the case and that there are rewards for obeying, your pup will accept this position without any problem.

You may notice that some dogs will sit very quickly, but will respond to the down command more slowly. This is their way of saying that they will obey the command, but under protest!

Staffordshire pups learn some of their behaviors from their parents or older dogs. If your adult dog has good manners, they will be passed on to your puppy.

Your dog should not be distracted during training. Make sure that he is focused on his lessons so that he learns properly.

There are two ways to teach this command. Obviously, with a puppy, it will be easier to teach the down if you are kneeling next to him. If your dog is more willing to please, the first method should work: Have your dog sit and hold a treat in front of his nose. When his full attention is on the treat, start to lower the treat slowly to the ground, saying "Down." The pup should follow the treat with his head. Bring it out slowly in front of him. If you are really lucky, your puppy will slide his legs forward and lie down by himself. Give the treat and lots of praise for being such a good dog. For a dog that won't lie down on his own (and most puppies won't), you can try this method: After the puppy is sitting and focused on the treat, take the front legs and gently sweep them forward, at the same time saying, "Down." Release the legs and quickly apply light pressure on the shoulders with your left hand. Then quickly tell the dog how good he is, give the treat, and make a lot of fuss. Repeat two or three times only in one training session. The pup will learn over a few lessons. Remember that this is a very submissive act on the pup's behalf, so there is no need to rush matters.

The Heel Command

All dogs should be able to walk nicely on a leash without a tug-of-war with their owners. Teaching your puppy the heel command should follow leash training. Heeling is best done in a place where you have a wall or a fence to one side of you, because it will restrict the puppy's movements so that you only have to contend with forward and backward situations. Again, it is better to do the lesson in private and not in a place where there will be many distractions.

There will be no need to use a slip collar on your puppy, as you can be just as effective with a flat, buckle one. The leash should be approximately 6 feet long. You can adjust the space between you, the puppy, and the wall so that your pet has only a small amount of room to move sideways. It is also very helpful to have a treat in your hand so that your dog will be focused on you and stay by your side.

Hold the leash in your right hand and pass it through your left. As the puppy moves ahead and pulls on the leash, give a quick jerk backward with your left hand, while at the same time saying "Heel." You want the pup's head to be at, but not touching, your knee. When the puppy is in this position, praise him and begin walking again. Repeat the whole exercise. Once the puppy begins to get the message, you can use your left hand (with the treat inside of it) to pat the side of your knee so that the pup is encouraged to keep close to your side.

THE GUIDE TO OWNING A STAFFORDSHIRE BULL TERRIER

The down command may be challenging for your Staffordshire to obey. The down position is a sign of submission in the dog world.

When the pup understands the basics, you can mix up the lesson a little to keep the dog focused. Do an about-turn, or make a quick left or right. This will result in a sudden jerk as you move in the opposite direction. The puppy will now be behind you, so you can pat your knee and say "Heel." As soon as the pup is in the correct position, give him lots of praise. The puppy will now begin to associate certain words with certain actions. When not in the heel position, your dog will experience discomfort as you jerk the leash. When the pup is along side of you, he will receive praise. Given these two options, your dog will always prefer the praise.

Once the lesson is learned and the dog is heeling reliably, then you can change your pace from a slow walk to a quick one, and the puppy will come to adjust. The slow walk is always the more difficult for most puppies, as they are usually anxious to be on the move. End the lesson when the pup is walking nicely beside you. Begin the lesson with a few sit commands so you're starting with success and praise.

Recall to Heel Command

When your puppy is coming to the heel position from an off-leash situation—for instance, if he has been running free—he should do this in the correct manner. He should pass behind you and take up his position, then sit. To teach this command, have the pup in front of you in the sit position with his collar and leash on. Hold the leash in your right hand. Give him the command to heel and pat your left knee. As the pup starts to move forward, use your right hand to guide him behind you. If you need to, you can hold the collar and walk the dog around the back of you to the desired position. You will need to repeat this a few times until the puppy understands what is wanted.

When you have done this a number of times, you can try it without the collar and leash. If the pup comes up toward your left side, then bring him to the sit position in front of you. Hold his collar and walk the pup around the back of you. Your dog will eventually understand and auto-matically pass around your back each time. If the dog is already behind you when you recall him, then the pup should automatically come to your left side. If necessary, pat your left leg.

The No Command

The no command must be obeyed every time. Your puppy must understand it 100 percent. Most delinquent dogs—the jumpers, the barkers, and the biters—have never been taught this command. If your puppy were to approach any potential danger, the no command, coupled with the come command, could save his life. You do not need a specific lesson for this command; it will most likely be used every day. You must be consistent and apply it every time your dog is doing something wrong. It is best, however, to be able to replace the negative command with something positive. This way, your puppy will respond quicker. For example, if your puppy is chewing on your shoe, tell him, "No!" and replace the shoe with a toy. Then give him lots of praise.

Showing Your Staffordshire Bull Terrier

A show dog is a comparatively rare thing. He is one dog out of several litters of puppies. He happens to be born with a degree of physical perfection that closely approximates the standard by which the breed is judged in the show ring. Such a dog should, on maturity, be able to win or approach his championship in good, fast company at the larger shows. Upon finishing his championship, he is apt to be as highly desirable as a breeding animal. As a proven stud, he will automatically command a high price for service.

Showing dogs is a lot of fun, but it is also a highly competitive sport. While all the experts were once beginners, the odds are against a novice. You will be showing against experienced handlers, often people who have devoted a lifetime to breeding, picking the right dogs, and then showing them through to their championships. Moreover, the most perfect dog ever born has faults, and in your hands the faults will be far more evident than with the experienced handler who knows how to minimize them. These are but a few points on the difficult side of the picture.

The experienced handler, as I say, was not born knowing the ropes. He learned—*and so can you!* You can succeed if you put in the same effort, study, and keen observation that he did. But it will take time!

KEY TO SUCCESS

First, search for a truly fine show prospect. Take the puppy home, raise him by the book, and as carefully as you know how, give him every chance to mature into the dog you hoped for. My advice is to keep your dog out

When starting out, visit dog shows without your dog and ask other owners about their show experiences. Their advice can help improve your performance.

of big shows, even Puppy Classes, until he is mature. Maturity in the male is roughly at 2 years of age; in the female, 14 months or so. When your dog is approaching maturity, start him out at match shows. With this experience, you can then go gunning for the big wins at the big shows.

Next, read the standard by which the breed is judged. Study it until you know it by heart. Having done this, and while your puppy is at home (where he should be) growing into a normal, healthy dog, attend every dog show you possibly can. Sit at the ringside and watch Staffordshire Bull Terrier judging. Keep your ears and eyes open. Do your own judging,

holding each of those dogs against the standard, which you now know inside out.

In your evaluations, don't start looking for faults. Look for the virtues—the best qualities. How does a given dog shape up against the standard? Having looked for and noted the virtues, then note the faults and see what prevents a given dog from standing correctly or moving well. Weigh these faults against the virtues, since, ideally, every feature of the dog should contribute to the harmonious whole dog.

RINGSIDE JUDGING

It's a good practice to make notes on each dog, always holding the dog against the standard. In "ringside judging," forget your personal preference for this or that feature. What does the standard say about it? Watch carefully as the judge places the dogs in a given class. From the ringside, it is sometimes difficult to see why number one was placed over the second dog. Try to follow the judge's reasoning. If possible, try to talk with him after judging is finished. Ask him questions as to why he placed certain dogs and not others. Listen carefully while the judge explains his placings—I'll say right here, any judge worthy of his license should be able to give sound reasons.

When you're not at the ringside, talk with the fanciers who have

Familiarize yourself with the breed standard if you plan on showing your dog.

Show dogs sometimes need to learn special stances and tricks. Take your time to train him according to what is expected.

Staffordshire Bull Terriers. Don't be afraid to ask opinions or say that you don't know. It will help you a great deal and speed up your personal progress if you are a good listener.

THE NATIONAL CLUB

You will find it worthwhile to join the national Staffordshire Bull Terrier club and to subscribe to its magazine. From the national breed club, you will learn the location of an approved regional club near Staffordshire Bull Terrier is eight to ten months old, find out the dates of match shows in your section of the country. They differ from regular shows only in that no championship points are given. These shows are especially designed to launch young dogs (and new handlers) on a show career.

ENTER MATCH SHOWS

With the ring deportment you have watched at big shows firmly in mind and in practice, enter your dog in as many match shows as you can. In the ring, you have two jobs. One is to see to it that your dog is always being seen to his best advantage. The other job is to keep your eye on the judge to see what he may want you to do next. Watch only the judge and your dog. Be quick and be alert; do exactly as the judge directs. Don't speak to him except to answer his questions. If he does something you don't like, don't say so. Also, don't irritate the judge (and everybody else) by constantly talking and fussing with your dog.

In moving about the ring, remember to keep clear of dogs beside you or in front of you. It is my advice to you *not* to show your Staffordshire Bull Terrier in a regular point show until he is at least close to maturity and after both you and your dog have had time to perfect ring manners and poise in the match shows.

Your Healthy Staffordshire Bull Terrier

All dogs, including Staffordshire Bull Terriers, are capable of contracting numerous health problems and diseases. Most of those problems can be avoided by adhering to responsible breeding practices. When only healthy and sound dogs are bred, many hereditary diseases can be avoided. Also, regular health maintenance and good general care can go a long way to keeping your dog healthy.

Your Staffordshire Bull Terrier should receive regular physical examinations or checkups from your veterinarian, starting when he is a puppy. You should also perform regular examinations of your dog yourself, paying attention to his skin, coat, eating habits, and demeanor. Any change should be reported to your veterinarian. A good relationship between you and your dog can make all the difference in his health.

VACCINATIONS

Every puppy, purebred or mixed breed, should be vaccinated against the major canine diseases. These are distemper, leptospirosis, hepatitis, and canine parvovirus. Your pup may have received a temporary vaccination against distemper before you purchased him, but ask the breeder to be sure.

The age at which vaccinations are given can vary, but will usually be when the pup is 8 to 12 weeks old. By this time, any protection given to the pup by antibodies received from his mother via her initial milk feedings will be losing their strength.

The puppy's immune system works on the basis that the white blood cells engulf and render harmless attacking bacteria. However, they must first recognize a potential enemy.

Vaccines are either dead or live bacteria, but in very small doses.

Vaccinating your puppy is essential. His immunity decreases once he is separated from his mother and her milk feedings.

Either type prompts the pup's defense system to attack them. When a large attack comes (if it does), the immune system recognizes it and massive numbers of lymphocytes (white blood corpuscles) are mobilized to counter the attack. However, the ability of the cells to recognize these dangerous viruses can diminish over a period of time. It is therefore useful to provide annual reminders about the nature of the enemy. This is done by means of booster injections that keep the immune system on its alert. Immunization is not 100 percent guaranteed successful, but is very close to it. Certainly, it is better than giving the puppy no protection.

Dogs are subject to other viral attacks, and if they are of a high-risk factor in your area, your vet will suggest that you have the puppy vaccinated against these as well.

Your puppy or dog should also be vaccinated against the deadly rabies virus. In fact, in many places it is illegal for your dog not to be vaccinated. This is to protect your dog, your family, and the rest of the animal population from a deadly virus that infects the nervous system and causes dementia and death.

FIGHTING FLEAS

Fleas are very mobile and may be red, black, or brown in color. The adults suck the blood of the host, while the larvae feed on the feces of the adults, which is rich in blood. Flea "dirt" may be seen on the pup as very tiny clusters of blackish specks that look like freshly ground pepper. The eggs of fleas may be laid on the puppy, though they are more commonly laid off of the host in a favorable place, such as the bedding. They normally hatch in 4 to 21 days, depending on the temperature, but they can survive for up to 18 months if temperature conditions are not favorable. The larvae are maggot-like and molt a couple of times before forming pupae, which can survive long periods until the temperature, or the vibration of a nearby host, causes them to emerge and jump on a host.

There are a number of effective treatments available. You should discuss them with your veterinarian, then follow all instructions for the one you choose. Any treatment will involve a product for your puppy or dog and one for the environment, and will require diligence on your part to treat all areas and thoroughly clean your home and yard until the infestation is eradicated.

THE TROUBLE WITH TICKS

Ticks are arthropods of the spider family, which means they have eight legs (though the larvae have six). They bury their headparts into the host and gorge on its blood. Ticks are easily

Dogs that play outside can pick up fleas and ticks. Inspect your dogs coat after playtime to make sure that he is free of external parasites.

If you have to leave your dog outside while you are away, leave some chew toys to keep him occupied. Also, having a dog house can give him some protection if he gets caught outside in bad weather.

seen as small grain-like creatures sticking out from the skin. They are often picked up when dogs play in fields, but may also arrive in your yard via wild animals, even birds, or stray cats and dogs. Some ticks are species-specific, others are more adaptable and will host on many species.

The most troublesome type of tick is the deer tick, which spreads the deadly Lyme disease that can cripple a dog (or a person). Deer ticks are tiny and very hard to detect. Often, by the time they're big enough to notice, they've been feeding on the dog for a few days—long enough to do their damage. Lyme disease was named for the area of the US in which it was first detected—Lyme, Connecticut—but has now been diagnosed in almost all parts of the US. Your veterinarian can advise you of the danger to your dog(s) in your area, and may suggest your dog be vaccinated for Lyme. Always go over your dog with a fine-toothed flea comb when you come in from walking through any area that may harbor deer ticks. Also, if your dog is acting unusually sluggish or sore, seek veterinary advice.

Attempts to pull a tick free will invariably leave the headpart in the pup, where it will die and cause an infected wound or abscess. The best way to remove ticks is to dab a strong saline solution on them, or to use iodine or alcohol. This will numb them, causing them to loosen their hold, at which time they can be removed with tweezers. The wound can then be cleaned and covered with an antiseptic ointment. If ticks are common in your area, consult with your vet for a suitable pesticide to be used in kennels, on bedding, and on the puppy or dog.

INSECTS AND OTHER OUTDOOR DANGERS

There are many biting insects, such as mosquitoes, that can cause discomfort to a puppy. Many diseases are transmitted by the males of these species. A pup can easily get a grass seed or thorn lodged between his pads or in the folds of his ears. These may go unnoticed until an abscess forms.

This is where your daily check of the puppy or dog will do a world of good. If your puppy has been playing in long grass or places where there may be thorns, pine needles, wild animals, or parasites, the checkup is a wise precaution.

SKIN DISORDERS

Apart from problems associated with lesions created by biting pests, a puppy may fall foul to a number of other skin disorders. Examples are

Keep an eye on your dog when he is outside playing. If he should become injured while playing, take him to your vet immediately.

Regular grooming sessions allow you to examine your dog's coat and skin for any problems.

ringworm, mange, and eczema. Ringworm is not caused by a worm, but is a fungal infection. It manifests itself as a sore-looking bald circle. If your puppy should have any form of bald patches on him, let your veterinarian check him over; a microscopic examination can confirm the condition. Many old remedies for ringworm exist, such as iodine, carbolic acid, formalin, and other tinctures, but modern drugs are superior.

Fungal infections can be very difficult to treat, and even more difficult to eradicate, because of the spores. These can withstand most treatments, other than burning, which is the best thing to do with bedding once the condition has been confirmed.

Mange is a general term that can be applied to many skin conditions where the hair falls out and a flaky crust develops and falls away.

Often, dogs will scratch themselves, and this invariably is worse than the original condition, because it opens lesions that are then subject to viral, fungal, or parasitic attack. The cause of the problem can be various species of mites. They either live on skin debris and hair follicles, which they destroy, or they bury themselves just beneath the skin and feed on the tissue. Applying general remedies from pet stores is not recommended because it is essential to identify the type of mange before a specific treatment can be effective.

Eczema is another nonspecific term applied to many skin disorders. The condition can be brought about in many ways. Sunburn, chemicals, allergies to foods, drugs, pollens, and stress can all produce a deterioration of the skin and coat. Given the range of causal factors, treatment can be difficult because the problem is one of identification. It is a case of taking each possibility and trying to correctly diagnose the matter. If the cause is of a dietary nature, you must remove one item at a time in order to find out if the dog is allergic to a given food. It could, of course, be the lack of a nutrient that is the problem, so if the condition persists, you should consult your veterinarian.

INTERNAL DISORDERS

It cannot be overstressed that it is very foolish to attempt to diagnose an internal disorder without the advice of a veterinarian. Take a relatively common problem such as diarrhea. It might be caused by nothing more serious than the puppy hogging a lot of food or eating something that he has never previously eaten. Conversely, it could be the first indication of a potentially fatal disease. It's up to your veterinarian to make the correct diagnosis.

The following symptoms, especially if they accompany each other or are progressively added to earlier symptoms, indicate that you should visit the veterinarian right away.

Continual Vomiting. All dogs vomit from time to time, and this is not necessarily a sign of illness. They will eat grass to induce vomiting. It is a natural cleansing process common to many carnivores. However, continued vomiting is a clear sign of a problem. It may be a blockage in the pup's intestinal tract, it may be induced by worms, or it could be due to any number of diseases.

Diarrhea. Diarrhea may be nothing more than a temporary condition due to many factors. Even a change of home can induce diarrhea, because this often stresses the pup, and invariably there is some change in the diet. If it persists more than 48 hours, something is amiss. If blood is seen in the feces, waste no time at all in taking your dog to the vet.

Running Eyes and/or Nose. A pup might have a chill, and this will cause the eyes and nose to weep. This should quickly clear up if the puppy is placed in a warm environment and away from any drafts. If it does not, and especially if a mucous discharge

Lots of love and attention will make your Staffordshire become your best friend. Take care of him properly and he'll be with you for a long time.

is seen, the pup has an illness that must be diagnosed.

Coughing. Prolonged coughing is a sign of a problem, usually of a respiratory nature.

Wheezing. If the pup has difficulty breathing and makes a wheezing sound when breathing, something is wrong.

Cries When Attempting to Defecate or Urinate. This might only be a minor problem due to the hard state of the feces, but it could be more serious, especially if the pup cries when urinating.

Cries When Touched. Obviously, if you do not handle a puppy with care, he might yelp. However, if he cries even when lifted gently, he has an internal problem that becomes apparent when pressure is applied to a given area of the body. Clearly, this must be diagnosed.

Refuses Food. Generally, puppies and dogs are greedy creatures when it comes to feeding time. Some might be more fussy, but none should refuse more than one meal. If they go for a number of hours without showing any interest in their food, then something is not as it should be.

General Listlessness. All puppies have their off days when they do not seem their usual cheeky, mischievous selves. If this condition persists for more than two days, there is little doubt of a problem. They may not show any of the signs listed, other than perhaps a reduced interest in their food. There are many diseases that can develop internally without displaying obvious clinical signs. Blood, fecal, and other tests are needed in order to identify the disorder before it reaches an advanced state that may not be treatable.

WORMS

There are many species of worm, and a number of these live in the tissues of dogs and most other animals. Many create no problem at all, so you are not even aware they exist. Others can be tolerated in small levels, but become a major problem if they number more than a few. The most common types seen in dogs are roundworms and tapeworms. While roundworms are the greater problem, tapeworms require an intermediate host and so are more easily eradicated.

Roundworms of the species *Toxocara canis* infest the dog. They may grow to a length of 8 inches (20 cm) and look like strings of spaghetti. The worms feed on the digesting food in the pup's intestines. In chronic cases, the puppy will become pot-bellied, have diarrhea, and vomit. Eventually, he will stop eating, having passed through the stage when he always seems hungry. The worms lay eggs in the puppy, and these pass out in his feces. They are then either ingested by the pup, or they are eaten by mice, rats, or beetles. These may, in turn, be eaten by the puppy, and the life cycle is complete.

Larval worms can migrate to the womb of a pregnant bitch, or to her mammary glands, and this is how they pass to the puppy. The pregnant bitch can be wormed, which will help. The pups can, and should, be wormed when they are about two weeks old. Repeat worming every 10 to 14 days and the parasites should be removed. Worms can be extremely dangerous to young puppies, so you should be sure your pup is wormed as a matter of routine.

Tapeworms can be seen as tiny rice-like eggs sticking to the puppy's or dog's anus. They are less destructive, but still undesirable. The eggs are eaten by mice, fleas, rabbits, and other animals that serve as intermediate hosts. They develop into a larval stage, and the host must then be eaten by the dog in order to complete the chain. Your vet will supply a suitable remedy if tapeworms are seen or suspected. The vet can also do an egg count on the pup's feces under the microscope; this will indicate the extent of an infestation.

There are other worms, such as hookworms and whipworms, that are also blood suckers. They will make a pup anemic, and blood might be seen in the feces, which can be examined by the vet to confirm their presence. Cleanliness in all matters is the best preventative measure for all worms.

BLOAT (GASTRIC DILATATION)

This condition has proved fatal in many dogs, especially large and deep-chested breeds. However, any dog can get bloat. It is caused by gases building up in the stomach, or especially in the small intestine. What happens is that carbohydrates are fermented and release gases. Normally, these gases are released by belching or by being passed from the anus. If for any reason these exits become blocked (such as if the stomach twists due to physical exertion), the gases cannot escape and the stomach simply swells and places pressure on other organs, sometimes cutting off the blood supply to the heart or causing suffocation. Death can easily follow if the condition goes undetected.

The best preventative measure is not to feed large meals or exercise your puppy or dog immediately after he has eaten. You can reduce the risk of flatulence by feeding more fiber in the diet, not feeding too many dry biscuits, and possibly by adding activated charcoal tablets to the diet.

ACCIDENTS

All puppies will get their share of bumps and bruises due to the rather energetic way they play. These will

A fenced-in yard will keep your dog from roaming the neighborhood—and getting into trouble.

usually rectify themselves over a few days. Small cuts should be bathed with a suitable disinfectant and then smeared with an antiseptic ointment. If a cut looks more serious, stem the flow of blood with a towel or makeshift tourniquet and rush the pup to the veterinarian. Never apply so much pressure to the wound that it might restrict the flow of blood to the limb.

In the case of burns, you should apply cold water or an ice pack to the surface. If the burn was due to a chemical, it must be washed away with copious amounts of water. If necessary, apply an antiseptic ointment to the burn. Trim away the hair if need be. Wrap the dog in a blanket, and rush him to the vet. The pup may go into shock, depending on the severity of the burn, and this will result in a lowered blood pressure, which is dangerous and the reason the pup must receive immediate veterinary attention.

If a broken limb is suspected, try to keep the animal as still as possible. Wrap your pup or dog in a blanket to restrict movement and get him to the veterinarian as soon as possible. Do not move the dog's head so that it is tilting backward, as this might result in blood entering the lungs.

Do not let your pup jump up and down from heights, because this can cause considerable shock to the joints. Like all youngsters, puppies do not know when enough is enough, so you must do all of their thinking for them.

Provided you apply strict hygiene to all aspects of your puppy's husbandry, and you make daily checks on his physical state, you have done as much as you can to safeguard him during his most vulnerable period. Routine visits to your veterinarian are also recommended, especially while the puppy is under one year of age. The vet may notice something that did not seem important to you.

Resources

Straffordshire Bull Terrier Club, Inc.
Secretary: Ralph Trenka
2298 Highway 142
Goldendale, WA 98620
clubs.akc.org/sbtci
Email: Rtrenka@aol.com

American Kennel Club
Headquarters:
260 Madison Avenue
New York, NY 10016

Operations Center:
5580 Centerview Drive
Raleigh, NC 27606-3390

Customer Services.
Phone: (919) 233-9767
Fax: (919) 816-3627
www.akc.org

The Kennel Club
1 Clarges Street
London
W1J 8AB
Phone: 087 0606 6750
Fax: 020 7518 1058
www.the-kennel-club.org.uk

The Canadian Kennel Club
89 Skyway Avenue
Suite 100
Etobicoke, Ontario, Canada
M9W 6R4
Order Desk & Membership:
1-800-250-8040
Fax: (416) 675-6506
www.ckc.ca

The United Kennel Club, Inc.
100 E. Kilgore Road
Kalamazoo, MI 49002-5584
(616) 343-9020
www.ukcdogs.com

07982 318532

Index

Photo Credits

Karen Taylor, pp. 15, 32
All other photos by Isabelle Francais